to mom and dad

*In memory of our loving mom
and "baba"*

1946 - 2020

*In memory of our loving dad
and "Papa Jack"*

1937 - 2020

Bravery is the pathway to joy.

beyondbrave.
by jolynn swafford

BRAVE AGAIN

Introduction

I am writing this book about the steps and how to be brave again after loss, unemployment, divorce, trauma, and addiction. This book tells my story and offers practical advice for other people who have been through difficult times in their life. I hope that this book will help others find peace in themselves enough to know that they can become brave again too.

It is just a matter of where we can find that bravery. Some people may have to dig deep into their soul for it, while others might find some in the little moments they share with loved ones or strangers during difficult times.

I started thinking about bravery and realize it is the trigger point to get us to the pathway to joy; I believe deep down inside is what we all truly desire.

I believe at some point in our lives, we all start brave. When we are born, we aren't programmed yet; we're not conditioned yet, we haven't failed yet, we are already perfect. There are no expectations on our life when we are born except to breathe and stay alive!

As life goes on, we begin to fall; other people project their expectations on us, we face trials and suffering and begin to lose that fierce, innate warrior bravery with which we are born.

Bravery is the key to getting us back on track. We all have some type of fear, but we know what it feels like to be brave too! When you're able to remember those moments in your life where you were so bold and brave, then I believe whatever problem or area of your life seems dark right now can take a turn for the better because, once again, there's nothing more potent than being brave again.

There is nothing more <u>potent</u> than being <u>brave.</u>

beyondbrave.
by jolynn swafford

Why Bravery?

Bravery is the intersection we must cross to get to the pathway to joy; which I believe deep down inside is what we all truly desire. I like to say that bravery is that point of transcendence, or upward journey, towards joy and enlightenment that "ends the trance"!

When my parents died last year, my life and the meaning of life shifted dramatically. While it was a sad tragedy for our family and me, it was a blessing because the experience truly emptied me. I will elaborate on this more in this book but suffice it to say; there was a point in these 60 days that nothing mattered more than loving my mother the way God does. In my journey, I had to put all of my needs aside to love her more than ever before.

The most challenging moment in my life brought me back full circle to being brave again. I found bravery through immense love and sacrifice. I found true joy in my suffering.

Recently, I shared this story with the Chief of one of the largest Native American Tribal Nations. He asked if I had a website or information on my journey to share with his loved ones because they had just endured something similar. At that moment, I decided to write this book for his family, and I as thought about what I'm teaching here --- **it's how to become Brave Again**.

It's no wonder the idea of bravery can seem elusive! We are told to be brave, but how do we do that? I needed some answers or at least someone who could show me their process for being brave again as I had become discouraged by my circumstances at multiple points in my life. That led me to study joy and bravery extensively. I wanted to share my knowledge and journey with you and my loved ones; hence this book "Brave Again" was created. BRAVE AGAIN - Restoring Your Life After Loss will help anyone looking for courage and inspiration after suffering loss. The book provides practical tools, spiritual guidance, and inspirational stories that will lift your spirit again.

The title itself speaks volumes because, in two words, you are reminded that there may always exist some level of fear within you. At any given moment, with just one step towards bravery, you can change everything and tap into your innate gift of fearlessness.

With just one step towards _bravery_ you can change _everything_.

beyondbrave.
by jolynn swafford

Going Beyond Brave

After my parents left this earth, I founded a company and called it Beyond Brave Co. The inspiration came from the saddest, greatest trial of my life. You see, I thought I had suffered enough already! Have you ever felt like that? Like you just keep getting knocked down?

I truly believed that the trials that I had already endured in my life were enough! I survived being gang-raped at age 14, which led me to a long downward spiral of promiscuity, alcoholism, and chemical dependency, which also resulted in not meeting my expectations. I used to look in the mirror every morning and say, "you're such a loser."

In 2014, I was diagnosed with liver failure, which was causing heart problems as well. My doctors gave me a choice "quit drinking or die." That was it. I stopped drinking that day. In 2016, I had the clarity to start improving my life:

I started reading personal development books

I traveled the world with Tony Robbins

Built my faith and relationship back up with God

Quit the career that was no longer bringing me joy

Forgave the men who assaulted me

I started a life coaching business so I could help others

I moved to the beach in Southern California

Life was good!

Then, my parents died. Both of my parents passed away within 60 days of each other unexpectedly. Our dad died of complications from Covid, and our mom and hero (momma) died from complications stemming from a rare degenerative brain disease. While mom had been declining for a while, we were not expecting her to leave us that soon.

I spent the last 30 days with my momma. She had several falls after insisting on living at home alone for as long as possible. Her last fall was tragic for her. She was down on the floor in her bathroom without help for over 23 hours: no food, water, or phone. After realizing we hadn't seen movement in the cameras in the house, we called 911. That is when the last 30 days started.

In those 30 days, I served her endlessly. Deep down, I knew she was dying, making her final transition. My faith and knowing of God's love told me to spend those days loving her as Jesus loved us. I wanted her to feel God's immense love on earth in her last days, and while I could not possibly show her that kind of love as a human, I knew from studying Jesus, all I had to do was love her more than I loved myself.

Sacrifice was my new way of loving her. At one point, I went three days on about 3 hours of sleep and about 300 calories of food each day. But my love for her, this desire to love her as God loves us, required sacrifice. I never felt fear, and although sometimes darkness would tell me that I was alone, I knew I was never alone. We are never alone.

I demonstrated my love for her by giving her sponge baths, feeding her the foods she loved (mostly chocolate), washing her feet. I would put lavender oils in the marks of a cross as if anointing her feet (like Mary did with Jesus). I prayed over her. I held her. I slept with her. I played along with her hallucinations. I acted like the person she thought I was (sometimes, she thought I was someone else). I was so tired. But God filled me with bravery. I was filled with a different energy.

I never knew love like this before!

I found that this sacrifice filled my soul. In the darkest, saddest moment of my life, my mother left me a gift. She served as the conduit to emptying me so that the Holy Spirit could fill me up. She was the ultimate mother to me up until her last breath.

I never knew love like this before!

After she transitioned to heaven, I returned home - exhausted and emotional. The loss was too much to bear. In addition to all of this, my business had suffered. I was operating as a solo life coach. During these months, I didn't bring in any sales or revenue; debt was building up. I just wanted to stay in bed and binge Netflix and do nothing.

At this point, I had one decision to make:

Stay in bed or get out of bed.

Looking back, I see that we can achieve bravery by one choice, one decision at a time.

I decided to get out of bed.

Then as I sat in my office, I realized the things I was working towards and all the things I thought were important before - no longer mattered to me.

So, as a trained life coach, I knew I needed to ask myself quality questions. Turning inward is a quick path to suffering. So, I started asking myself, "how can I honor my parents' legacy?", "what would they want me to do?", "What lessons did they teach me?" and finally, "how can I take this suffering and help others?

I realized; our parents taught us how to be brave. They taught us that bravery is "putting more into the world than you take!"

They taught us to overcome fear and that we must persevere. And my parents never let us give up when things got severe or complicated. They showed us how to step out into the unknown with faith in what will come next. I knew my parents would want me to use this difficult time as a chance for transformation - not an excuse to stay stuck.

This book is about: how you can be brave again after loss, unemployment, divorce, trauma & addiction by making one decision at a time (the best way).

It starts by getting out of bed and looking back on your life's journey so far. This book shows you where you are now and helps you see your future from another perspective.

This book will inspire you if you are struggling in your life post-loss or other struggles, and if you aren't struggling, this book will prepare and equip you for future battles!

Let me remind you that your life has been a story of bravery. You are not alone in this journey!

Bravery is the <u>key</u> to getting us back on track.

beyondbrave.
by jolynn swafford

Bravery Versus Courage

Bravery is not just doing scary things. I want to share with you the difference between bravery and courage.

There are two main differences between courage and bravery.

The first difference is that bravery doesn't have to be related to fear. Bravery comes from a sense of duty or responsibility, like when someone holds their ground in the face of an overwhelming threat for the sake of others.

Courage and bravery are both often seen in soldiers on battlefields. Still, it's not always clear which one applies if they're doing something brave because they want to help other people - like carrying out a difficult order under fire - or just at risk themselves. However, courage usually refers to physical danger, while bravery would mean taking moral risks too.

Boldness is another word used for bravery; this might

sound similar but has different meanings depending on where you live! For instance, the Choctaw use the word "tushka," which means "warrior (bravery) for good."

In this book, when I refer to bravery, I am not referring to doing things like jumping out of a perfect airplane. That is what I consider as "courageous."

Courage means doing something despite fear.

My definition of bravery is doing something without fear for the benefit of others, even if that means you need to sacrifice something important to you. These acts of bravery are not for credit or recognition. They are selfless acts for others. Bravery does not have any emotional investment in personal gain or selfish goals.

The difference between courage and bravery is that you still must have a negotiation with "the ego" with courage." I will talk much more about "the ego" as we go along in this book. Just remember there is no negotiation when it comes to bravery. You "Just Do It," as Nike says (they were onto something!).

Also, courage doesn't require love, extreme love for other people necessarily. Courage still involves the ego.

Bravery, on the other hand, is a little different. Bravery requires both courage and love for others - not just yourself. You need to give up something that you cherish in your heart so that someone else can benefit from it as well.

"The ego" would say, "you're throwing away what's important!" The brave person will counter with, "I'm giving this gift of selflessness because I want to help."

The example many people think about when they hear the word bravery is Mother Theresa or Mahatma Gandhi, who sacrificed their own lives for others without hesitation even though they were living in poverty themselves at times. They had faith in humanity which enabled them to live wholly out of love!

Courage doesn't require any faith that believes in that which desired for yet to be seen. An example of this would be the first man on the moon. He had no faith in humanity, but he looked to his inner wisdom and courageously took that giant leap into space, trusting himself entirely for a triumphant return to earth.

Courage is not about sacrificing yourself or what you need; it's just getting out there and taking care of business!

Now let me share with you what bravery is! We are born with bravery. There is no psychological negotiation of "do I want to do this?", "do I not want to do this?", "Yeah, let's do it!", "let's go for it!" and then and only then you do it anyway. With bravery, none of that dialogue happens in your mind.

Bravery is the ability to do what you know in your heart and soul that's right for others! Bravery is not being scared and doing it anyway! It's having faith in yourself to do what you know is right.

What happens is that with bravery, we are taking action without any fear, and the reason we're able to take this action because we are warriors for good. We love other people so much that immense love overcomes any fear, and so there is no fear because you know that what you need to do must be done. After all, it's for the betterment of others. Bravery is more than the absence of fear; bravery is the presence of overwhelming love for others!

The loss of a loved one is devastating and changes everything. You'll never be the same again, but you can find happiness in your life again.

Loss is something that we will all endure in life. In this book, I talk a lot about losing a loved one; but these same practical tools will guide you through any loss (job, love, health, etc.).

The truth is if you love someone eventually, you will lose that person someday. I wouldn't say I like using the word "loss" because I don't feel like I lost my parents. Know exactly where they are. It's just a term that we use to share that familiar feeling. We are the ones that are lost.

We lost our dad due to complications from COVID. I could feel completely alone, but in fact, so many of us share this common bond. Please think of the millions of people who died from COVID complications, and whether you believe that COVID was a real thing or not, the truth is we all lost somebody during this same pandemic era.

So how do we collectively overcome this loss? How do we pick ourselves up and start living again? How do we pick up our feet and simply move forward after losing somebody we love? How do we peel ourselves out of bed from numbing out on Netflix?

Realize that you're not alone!

There is light and dark that exist in the world. This world is a battle of good versus evil, light versus dark, right versus wrong, you versus me, and in a lot of sense, it's a battle of "the ego." When you start to feel bad when you start to feel intense regret or guilt, which are feelings that we all have when we lose somebody we love, "the ego" is in overdrive. Let me give you some ideas of how you know that the ego is in overdrive:

You're feeling bad about yourself
Some thoughts keep spinning around in your head
You can't sleep because of intense regret or guilt

You're constantly feeling thoughts like I'm alone
You feel like you're the only person on the planet that's suffering right now
Ideas like "I don't deserve this" pop into your mind
You simply freeze; you can't move
You want to crawl into a dark hole stay in bed all day for weeks

I have a secret to share with you:

The ego is bravery's #1 enemy. The only reason the ego exists is to justify its existence! Did you know that at the very height of the scale of emotions (or Map of Consciousness by David Hawkins) is enlightenment and pure joy?

How do we become brave again? Become aware of your thoughts and become aware of "the ego" when speaking to you once you become aware of when you feel like you're the only person in the world regarding this pain, and once you can say to yourself, I am not alone! I couldn't possibly be alone! There are over 8 billion people on the planet! Just get outside of yourself long enough to realize how many people die every day, every single minute, and then every single second in the world - now, think about how somebody loved all those people!!! You can't possibly be alone! You can't be the only person who's ever experienced loss and pain in this world!

This is just one way to become brave again. First, become aware of your thoughts and be mindful of the ideas that fill your head when you feel like it's all too much. Notice when you start feeling like you are all alone or that nobody else has gone through anything quite as complicated as your situation. Then realize how many people do experience the same pain and suffering. Soon you will know that you are not alone.

I might be the only person who's ever lost a loved one in this specific way, but I am not alone. There are so many other people out there who have experienced loss and pain just like me. And that means it is possible to become brave again after difficult times - because we all can too!

Humans are so used to worry, fear, anxiety, remorse, guilt, conflict, and distress that they are accepted as normal life. We are then advised to seek a therapist to "get in touch with our feelings."

The truth is that a normal state of consciousness is one filled with joy and love.

This is our normal state.

This is how we are born!

Anything else is just an illusion.

Society tends to see this state of joy and love as something artificially produced!

After my parents died, I was still able to show up strong, full of love and joy, and serving others. Some people even tried to tell me I was delusional! I even had a few people tell me that I manufactured my joy to help me cope with my loss.

The truth is that I had worked my bravery and joy muscles for so long that it became my natural state. Bravery is now my emotional home, and it can be yours too. Imagine that.

The ego is the enemy of bravery.

beyondbrave.
by jolynn swafford

Bravery Means Letting Go

Surrendering Control

Sometimes, we must let go of the way things used to be. When all paths seem lost and impossible, sometimes it's time to surrender.

If you're in a situation where letting go seems impossible or out of your control--and that feeling will linger for some time after beginning this process--it may take practice before you can fully put these ideas into action. I know because I could barely move past my feelings at first either.

When people are going through difficult times, they often experience how painful letting go and realize how important it is. If there's any advice I can give with the hope of easing your pain, then here goes: don't hold on so tight; stop gripping onto the thing you can see. Instead, take each day as it comes. Each moment is a chance to start fresh and experience something beautiful.

It's okay if you're not ready to let go today, but I encourage you to think about the possibility of peace in your future--even if that seems like an impossible goal at this time. What are some small things you can do right now to feel empowered?

Let me share a story about my scooter, "Valentina the Vespa" (note that Valentina means "brave" in Italian"). The day after I got the Vespa, I took "her" out for a simple ride to the grocery store. Everything was terrific until two things happened: 1) I saw a speed bump and wanted to avoid it because I was unsure about it, and 2) I shifted into fear and lost control of the scooter.

Now let me explain. I first lost my balance, which caused fear to kick in, and then naturally (since I felt like I was falling off the bike), I grabbed onto the handlebars with all my might! Well, the problem with that is that the handlebars were also the throttle! The scooter sped up, and I ended up bouncing off cars in the parking lot like the ball inside a pinball machine! My fear of letting go was so intense that holding on started working against me! Fortunately, I ended up skidding into a parked car, and the scooter came to an abrupt stop.

The handlebars turned and stabbed into my chest. I was holding on so tightly for dear life! This experience was a powerful reminder that letting go is not only necessary but also brave. Letting go can be scary because it means trusting something or someone else with your safety - someone who may or may not have your best interests in mind. Depending on yourself by letting go of fear has nothing to do with self-esteem; it is about letting things take their natural course without controlling them all the time.

We are here on this earth for a limited time, and life is too short to spend worrying about everything that could happen, which might keep you from living as fully as possible.

Surrendering Your Motives

I understand better than anyone that we all need the motive to create change. The definition of motive is "a reason for doing something." It's essential to have a motive because it gives you the energy and focus needed to commit.

Sometimes we find ourselves in situations where our motives are no longer helpful; they're not enough anymore or don't work with how life has changed. When this happens, surrendering your original motives can be freeing- letting go of old ways is an act of bravery that will allow you to live again fully.

Remember, bravery is not just the absence of fear; it is the absence of self. We must surrender our motives for ourselves and let our reasons be for the good of others. By keeping motives just for your interest, you are limiting your future.

Surrendering Your Needs

Reflecting on taking care of my mother in her last days, letting go of my own needs was the single biggest shift of my life. I will admit, I wasn't selfish, but I sure did always have my needs in mind. As I was taking care of my mother, it took a toll on me physically and mentally. The lesson here is that letting go of our needs for ourselves will always be in the best interest of others. This last sacrifice can feel so freeing because we give up something that has been with us most of our life: being selfless or caring about only what's good for us.

When tragedy strikes your life, it changes everything; how you see things now versus previously seems like two different worlds. What once seemed important may no longer matter anymore, and what didn't seem all too significant then starts feeling more important than ever.

Taking care of my mother was extreme work. The ongoing process started feeling more draining than fulfilling—and that's when I knew it was time to let go of my needs.

Truthfully, it wasn't taking care of her that was so exhausting! It was trying to take care of her needs and my needs. So, once I let go of my own needs and tapped into the immense love I have for her, everything got more effortless; it was like magical energy took over from that point onward.

Bravery is knowing how to surrender and let go.

beyondbrave.
by jolynn swafford

Taming The Mind

A significant part of becoming brave again is to tame the mind. I can sleep feeling tremendous and dreaming big; sometimes, I can't sleep; I am so excited to wake up and start the new day.

Then, I wake up, and reality settles in. I start procrastinating, time goes by, and my mind starts in overdrive thinking: "How are you going to do that" "You don't have enough time," "You don't have enough knowledge or resources".... the mind thinks and thinks until I finally realize I got nothing done!

Sound familiar? In this chapter, I am going to share with you how to tame the mind.

Notice, firstly, that I refer to it as "the mind." The first thing to do is realize that the mind babbles and is seriously distracting. Bring your awareness to these thoughts, and if you try to organize them into some logical sequence, you will quickly learn that there is no intelligence behind these babbling thoughts.

Instead, start focusing on the desired action you want to take! Take brave action. The bold step that puts the needs of others first that shows unconditional love for others is a force for good.

The mind is not a warrior!

Your spirit is the warrior!

You must never forget this.

The second thing you must do is decrease the amount of time for contemplation. When you start over-contemplating, I want you to visualize an inner thinker responsible for organizing tons of thoughts, observations, associations, and conditioning from others into a file folder in mind. The term for this process is called mentation.

It is not about thinking more or better thoughts; it's about taking brave action! Bravery is putting your faith where the step is. The warrior does what needs to be done without hesitation. If you hesitate, then you are lost, and nothing will happen. Ignoring your intuition on this matter will only cause problems down the road, so do your best to always listen to your gut instinct and act fast when it tells you something!

It's essential to use your intuition and take responsibility for all of the thoughts in your mind. You are capable of making changes when you choose to release old ideas. Life is a process; it takes time to heal from difficult times. Stop putting yourself down because you think there is something wrong with you or feel like nothing will ever change! Remember, the events of the universe happens on its terms. Don't be surprised if things happen quickly without warning at any moment!

As one of my favorite spiritual teachers, David Hawkins, said, "One thing is obvious, the mind is unreliable and cannot be depended on at all. The mind is filled with society's emotions, frustrations, feelings, prejudices, blind spots, denials, projections, phobias, fears, regrets, guilts, worries, anxiety, and the fearsome specters of poverty, old age, sickness, death, failure, rejection, loss and disaster." He continues to day "the mind has been innocently and erroneously programmed by endless propaganda, political slogans, religious dogmas, and a continuous distortion of facts".

Now, let me put this into context for you. When my father called to tell us he had COVID, I was worried and angry. Everything on the news 24/7 was about COVID (as the virus was at its peak across the United States at the time). I realized I was getting angrier and angrier as time went on because the news was constantly talking about how unfair it was that loved ones and the patients could not see each other, and people were dying all alone. Then, a tough four weeks later, we decided to pull my father off the ventilator; he was gone in less than 15 seconds. This experience triggered so many emotions for me. I wanted to call the news stations and yell, "this is real! take care of yourselves!".

The months following the news continuously covered COVID, politics, religion, science all weighed in - there was a collective pain in the world about this. I started telling myself, "I'm a victim, every single time the news comes on, I feel like I'm experiencing this pain again and again!".

Then, I had an "ah-ha!" moment! Thankfully, my training, knowledge, and obsession about joy, bravery, and managing the mind and ego reminded me that I was only absorbing the thoughts of everyone on the television and news!

I knew better, and this still took over the mind!

Now, you know better too. But it is just a reminder that we must work this muscle all the time. "Bravery fitness" isn't an overnight sensation. We have to practice and practice. Remember that "repetition is the mother of skill," as my mentor and friend Tony Robbins says.

We must stop letting these thoughts live in our heads so that they take over the mind, body, and soul. What's important here is for you not to feel like a victim of circumstance or experience. You are only experiencing it because your mind has allowed you to! The best way to deal with dominant thoughts is to de-personalize the ideas and the mind. Begin practicing by calling it "the mind." In the beginning, I named the mind so that I could distance myself from it and even attempt to have conversations with it. I have these conversations regularly, and as I attempt to sort the thoughts out logically, the thoughts lose their power and dominance. As you practice this repeatedly, the thoughts will begin to lose control and domination; eventually, the thoughts will diminish faster and faster.

What is essential to understand is that this pathway through the mind and the ability to bypass the mind is necessary to become brave again. You must be mindful that the only reason the mind clings onto these thoughts is that the ego and its vanity declare them as "mine."

Another way to diminish the power and dominance of the mind is to step back and become the observer of these thoughts. I like to attach the thought onto the back of an imaginary airplane (like the ones with the signs attached to the back that fly over the crowded beaches). I do this and watch the thought pass right in front of me. Once it's gone and out of my imaginary sight - I've acknowledged the thought instead of "fighting" it.

Once you realize you are "fighting" or "killing" a thought, be mindful that this is the vanity of the ego back at work again. Any form of resistance will be the work of the ego and force the thought to persist even harder.

As I observe this thought, I like to ask the following questions, taken from "The Work" by the incredible Byron Katie.

Question 1: Is it true? This **question** can change your life. ...

Question 2: Can you absolutely know it's true? ...

Question 3: How do you react—what happens—when you believe that thought? ...

Question 4: Who would you be without the thought? ...

The **5th question** is my own: Is this thought useful?

"The Work" is a deceptively simple process that leads to profound spiritual awakening. Katie's four questions and turnarounds are designed to guide you past the mind's false belief systems into your understanding of who you are: completely loved, fearlessly beautiful, deeply connected with life. You'll be able to see what needs healing in your life; release all self-criticism; find relief from old wounds and painful memories; let go of resentment, jealousy, guilt--all feelings which may have been causing physical pain or mental anguish for years without your knowledge.

When we stop believing our thoughts about reality—what it means or doesn't mean—and start living bravely again, then liberation becomes possible.

Another way to quiet the mind is to surrender these motives to God:

1) The desire to think.

The mind seems to fear that it will disappear if it is silent, even for a moment. Practicing short and then more prolonged periods of silence (no music, guided meditation), just stillness and surrender will quiet the mind. Be still.

2) The desire for the pleasure of thinking.

The mind finds pleasure in keeping you in survival mode. If you begin to own the mind's thoughts, you begin to pat yourself on the back to think of all of the possible scenarios and build elaborate stories.

3) The comfort of the guarantee for the continuation of one's existence.

The mind and the ego exist merely to justify their existence. The more it thinks, the more it perpetuates its function. The mind becomes proud of holding onto these thoughts.

Have you ever noticed how the mind can create elaborate, lengthy stories when it goes into overdrive? As you focus on letting go of the motives behind overthinking, you will start catching these thoughts early in their formation!

Letting go is a great relief and will soon become a huge benefit. Can you imagine how it will feel to no longer be in bondage to the mind?!

To never again be controlled by thoughts of fear and worry?

To have a sense of "I am enough"?

To not feel the need for validation from others or external circumstances to feel loved, significant, or worthy?

As you practice letting go of this overthinking, you will notice that a sense of humility comes over you. When this happens, you become a willing receiver of God's power and energy and begin to see and feel God's unconditional love and presence.

This is how you practice being brave again: by letting go of dominance of the mind, the ego, and its false bravado. When we surrender to a higher power, release our attachments and fears while understanding that there's something much more extraordinary than us in all of this, we can be braver not just for ourselves but also with others.

Your spirit is the <u>warrior!</u>

beyondbrave.
by jolynn swafford

Humility and Bravery

As the ego starts to dissolve and the mind's thoughts start to lose power in your life, a new fear will develop. You will begin wondering, "how will I go on without the mind and these thoughts?" or "Wasn't I conditioned this way to keep me safe?"

Without going into the details of the human brain and how we have evolved over centuries, suffice it to say, we are no longer living in the same conditions that existed 100 years ago, much less 1,000 years ago or longer! Those thoughts no longer pertain to our modern society.

Secondly, if you've gone through the practice of asking the five questions I shared with you in the previous chapter, you will soon realize the ridiculousness of the thoughts, and I hope you find yourself laughing on occasion. Other questions that might arise are, "How will we eat today?" "How will life go on?"

Here is my secret. At this point, I love to ask myself,

"Who do you think you are?"

Seriously! Try it, "Who do you think you are?" Are you the Creator of the universe? Are you a unique divine power? Are you all-knowing, all present, all-seeing? This is a great time to humble yourself. Warriors are forces for good, and we are humble. Our humility allows us to admit our mistakes, realize our true limitations, and surrender. With humility, we can relinquish the ego's role as savior of the world and surrender it straight to God!

One important truth is that all fears are unfounded and not based on reality. Spiritual worries fade away when one meets and conquers this fear, liberating oneself from them to discover that these fears are without any basis.

For example, depending on what we are going through, we might experience a lot of guilt. Truthfully, guilt and blame are inevitable when you lose a loved one (or anything else for that matter). The mind starts thoughts like "You should have..." or "Why didn't you..." or "You should have noticed "... the guilt questions go on and on. The mind starts obsessing about all the things you should have done. In this instance, we must remember that this is just a part of a spiritual journey that requires relinquishing all of the beliefs and attitudes to create a new reality that shines forth with God's love for you.

The absence of ego allows for compassion and an open mind. We must let go of the need to be right. It is brave to admit that you are wrong! Remember that the need always to be right is the vanity of the ego at work and will prevent you from the joy that is your birthright.

Humility allows us to let go of the known for the unknown. Humility is an awareness of the limitations of the mind and appearance. The humility of the human being is in acknowledging that we are not perfect and do not always have all or even most of the answers.

There is a difference between humility and humiliation. Humility comes from awareness, while humiliation stems from a lack thereof. To be humiliated means to feel less-than; it's when you're made to feel inferior because someone thinks they know better than you do.

Humility requires us to move beyond who we think we are into our essence, which can only come about by understanding what God has created each of us for - greatness! It takes great bravery to allow yourself the opportunity to grow spiritually by admitting that there may be more out there than the ego wants you to believe. True humility requires great commitment, willingness, and devotion to surrendering our faith to God's will. This is the ultimate act of bravery because it entails relinquishing our will to a Higher Power.

The next step on your journey to recovery and becoming brave again, then, is humility. You must be willing to admit that you do not know how this experience truly relates to God's work in your life or what lessons are hidden within the difficult times you have experienced so far. Humility also requires an understanding that there may never be any suitable explanation for why such things happen--you can only surrender yourself wholly into His care without asking questions now. It takes faith and trust, as well as patience before you will reveal these beautiful gifts!

I love to say that bravery is the reliance on divine wisdom that makes allowances for our limitations. To truly be brave, humility is required.

Bravery is the reliance on <u>divine</u> wisdom that makes <u>allowances</u> for our limitations

beyondbrave.
by jolynn swafford

Bravery and Grieving

A key component of bravery that we must remember is that bravery does not mean bravado. You don't have to be tough and resilient all the time. Bravery is about facing life; it allows your emotions to flow and not worry about what others think.

Grief is incredibly unique. Grief and loss is a common experience; however, we all grieve differently in our way. While there is no "right" way to grieve, we can understand grief and how it looks for others.

Many people feel that things are too difficult when they go through a grieving process. They think that they will never make it, or they think nothing seems right. I remember after my parents died having thoughts like, "I wasted time." I felt so lonely and sad in this time of loss. The words "If only..." and hopelessness filled the mind as I tried to sleep at night. My mind continued to go back and forth between all the different things I would have done differently. It was all-consuming.

Meanwhile, right in front of me, I have an amazing husband, four beautiful, healthy children, three dogs, and a cat, and a long-awaited revived relationship with my older sister. So many things to be grateful for, but I simply couldn't focus on any of that. Feelings of abandonment, pain, helplessness, and hopelessness consumed me. There was this endless cycle of nostalgia, melancholy, depression, longing, heartbreak, anguish. My heart ached inside.

If you have experienced loss, you can probably relate, right? It's the feeling of "I'll never get over this." We cry out, hoping someone can help us, and our loved ones say things like "I wish I could take the pain away," but they can't, so then we are left feeling hopeless.

There is also this feeling of guilt. I remember feeling that if I were happy, then my parents would think I forgot about them. The mind will play so many tricks during grief!

It's not about the "how" because at some point, we have to move forward with our lives and do something else besides grieving - but we don't know where or how to start. Grief can be such an overwhelming emotion and feeling, so what is one supposed to do when faced with this? How can we possibly be brave?

Allow the Grieving to Happen

How can we be brave? What is bravery in the face of grief? Bravery isn't about feeling like you need to do something. It's more about doing what needs to get done. It means taking care of yourself and your family when no one else will or knows how. Bravery is asking for help from someone who has been in a similar place before. Being brave might mean getting some counseling if you feel stuck; sometimes, people want to talk it out with someone because they are afraid and alone without anyone around them who understands their pain.

Bravery doesn't have to take giant leaps all the time. But we do need to stop hiding our emotions of grief. Trust me, I am a woman who thinks positively and can accomplish just about anything, but even for me, some things are outside of my control. I am brave for sharing my story with you because it is the most daring thing I have ever done.

The grief journey can be demanding and sometimes confusing, but we need to accept what life throws at us, even if it's not exactly how we wanted things to go down. You will get through this, too, just like thousands of others before you who had a lot less in their lives than you do now. Keep going forward; there are people on your team rooting for you all along the way."

Many people have difficulty feeling their grief. Men, in particular, are often shamed into denying the expression of emotional hurt, and women are usually made to feel the need to suppress their anger (considering its generally seen as a masculine attribute). Sometimes we can't win!

Grieving after loss isn't just about grieving the "present" loss; it is an expression of grief of the accumulation of loss and sadness throughout our lives. I remember curling up into a ball next to my husband and finally saying, "I just want to cry, but it hurts to cry that hard".

I remember explicitly having another "ah-ha!" moment where I realized I am grieving all of the pain from my entire life, right here, right now! Grief is not linear and can be overwhelming at first without becoming more manageable over time. There are many facets to grief; from sorrowful feelings, dogs that I loved that died, the sadness of my best friend taking his own life, the sadness of moving away from my best friend in New Jersey, that time when my grandmother died and I never got to meet her, my divorce, my job loss, that time I went to jail and lost my dignity (another story for later)... and all those moments that had been bottled up inside me for years.

I was grieving everything! And it just felt like too much. I remember feeling so ashamed of myself because I couldn't control it; there wasn't any order to what came out when – anger followed by sadness or grief mixed in with guilt and depression. The pain would come out wherever it could find an outlet - sometimes waves of sobbing.

This is the accumulation of my grief, and this is what happens to all of us.

How To Move Forward

The ego and the mind will create a resistance to accepting grief and loss. It will start to say things like "You got this," "You're tough!", "You can do it", "You can handle this!".

The more we allow these thoughts to run our lives, the more harm is caused. This "resistance" results in illness and chronic health conditions or complaints. I can spot someone from a mile away holding onto grief, guilt, fear, and pain. Have you ever noticed that you can even see it as the expression on their face? Even the color of their skin? Do the eyes begin to look dull? It is as if their light was extinguished!

The story of grief is one that we all must know and understand. We are born into it, live in the midst of it for much, if not our whole lives, and then die from it. But there is always a way out! When we begin to see what grief does to us, how deeply rooted it goes within us, when we turn toward acceptance rather than resistance - this is the moment where transformation can happen.

I hope for you today: You will embrace your bravery again - brave enough to be vulnerable with yourself and others so that healing can once more occur. I pray that your family and friends will begin to notice a pep in your step, a vibrancy to your skin, and youth your eyes.

Becoming brave again allows us to release our emotions and speak freely of how we are feeling in the moment. We remove the need for approval and acceptance, and we are authentically true to how we are in that moment. We do not have any selfish motives; we do not need attention, we do not need consoling, we just need to speak our minds and cry when we need to.

It is time to grieve openly.

I hope you will not be scared to feel the full range of grief.

You are worthy and deserving of this space for your emotions, feelings, thoughts, memories, and dreams-- all that can bring a sense of closure back into life.

We often have an idea in our head about what we need to do when tragedy strikes us--to get over it or move on from it as quickly as possible. But I believe there needs to be time set aside where these tough times can genuinely touch each other with peace and kindness so we may come out stronger than before.

When we fully submit ourselves to the grief, it will exhaust quickly without making any other efforts. If we keep surrendering to it every time it comes up, then it will eventually run out. We only have to tolerate this grief 10-20 minutes at a time! Ultimately, it will disappear.

But if we resist the grief with "tough talk" and "at-a-boys" you can be assured it will persist for years!

Dealing With Attachment

The psychological basis of grief and mourning is attachment. This attachment and dependence occur because we feel incomplete within ourselves. Then we begin seeking other relationships, objects, people, events, places to fulfill these needs. In some cases, people will seek out substances or even risky behaviors.

One of the biggest shifts for me was when I stopped claiming ownership of my parents as "my mother" or "my father". By allowing and accepting the grieving process and my willingness to surrender to my Higher Power, I realized they were humans that never "belonged" to me. Therefore, they were not an extension of "me."

The truth is, all along, they have "belonged" to our Creator!

Once I realized this, I no longer feel an obligation to them or guilt. I also do not need to control and manage my parents' lives for fear of being abandoned in my grief. I now have a sense of freedom, peace, and relief that I was yearning for in this grief journey.

The fact that you've lost someone or something important to you does not diminish WHO you are!

We must work through the various emotions associated with mourning and loss. We need you to be brave because chronic guilt and the feelings associated with that will consume you if you don't. Bravery will help you release that suppressed sadness and energy so you can live a complete life!

There was a point I like to call the "window of grace," where I realized, if I do not deal with these emotions and let them flow through me, I will die.

I did not want to die. My family needs me, and I need them! A brave conviction inside me grew so intense that I started to say, "make this pain matter"; "help others." I started practicing the skill of allowing the emotions for a little while and letting go of the negative feelings. This became the cure for pain, and I started seeking out ways to give others (and myself) even more unconditional love.

I soon replaced the fear and sadness with trust and a profound sense of wellbeing. I felt brave again.

I found the happiness I had always wanted in loving

others. The world needs more brave people to show up and share their love with all those around them to live a full life again!

This is what has helped me become BRAVE AGAIN:

- feeling a sense of freedom to be me and openly talk about the person who died or left;

- realizing that grief will not last forever, but it's OKAY if it feels like this for a while. Life will go on once we are brave again;

- learning how to accept help from others when I need it and then giving back in my way after I've been through the process

Bravery is asking for help when you need it

beyondbrave.

by jolynn swafford

Get Your Joy Back!

So far, we have talked a lot about loss, grieving, the ego, and how to tame the mind. Now, I want you to know that I am 100% certain you can get your joy back too! Joy is the product of faith and a grateful heart. So, what does it mean to be grateful? Gratitude means you are thankful for all things in your life-from good times and bad.

To you to get your joy back, there are seven crucial things you must know about joy.

1) Joy is a mindset. Once you choose to live with that mindset, you can tap into your fullest potential. Joy is already within you. You were born with it. We just tend to have "joy interruptions" that keep us from staying in that place. Think of this new mindset as a new way of living. Joy is different than happiness. Joy is a mile deep and a mile wide.

Happiness is an inch deep and a mile wide. Happiness scratches the surface compared to joy. I think joy is just simply infinite, and it's something that can serve other people. It's contagious and long-lasting, whereas happiness is temporary. Probably the most critical difference is that we can lose happiness in an instant.

2) Happiness depends on external factors. Some of those factors you can't control. Joy is permanent and built from within. It is independent of external circumstances. I like to say that when you have joy, you don't need anything else. Everything else is a bonus.

The point is, we can find joy in the most unlikely places. It's a choice to get back that joy. It is possible to experience joy even in terrible circumstances but then somehow coming out stronger than before.

The accumulation of these struggles ended up being the most ultimate awakening experience for me – one where I discovered greater joy than ever before - finding out what matters to me: people, love (even though at times it feels like our world has turned into inhumanity) and nature.

No matter your story or where you are now, there is hope for finding joy again if you know how to look for it within yourself instead of looking outside. And one way we can find joy during tough times is through faith. As someone who has experienced hardship firsthand many times throughout my life, I have learned about the power of resilience and strength when they come together with bravery!

I have realized that the experience of joy is so much more about what we do with it than who has it. We can all find happiness in our way, and my life's work now focuses on helping others restore their lives after difficult times so they can get their joy back.

3) Where your focus goes, your energy flows. If you focus on the negative – you will experience more negative. You must focus on the potential opportunities and the anticipation of an unlimited future. And that's exciting, especially when you can apply faith. Living by faith and not by sight becomes a little bit of a game. Life becomes a fun little game instead of the battle of ups and downs. Joy reminds us to have more believe in an empowering future while having fun. Joy is flow.

So, take a moment and ask yourself: What brings me

lasting joy? And then go out there today and invest time into those things! The key to feeling good again lies inside us—and as long as we keep looking for ways to feel better in ourselves instead of running from discomfort or trying harder at something else, we will be able to make progress one day at a time.

4) Practice gratitude in different ways to awaken the true spirit of joy. Many people write in gratitude journals in the morning, which is excellent, but it's time to change when it starts to become a task. Also, be sure to practice gratitude all day, see the little things and the beauty all around you. Get your heart so deep in appreciation that you cry tears of joy just noticing the wonder all around you. That is true joy.

It's not always easy to maintain that gratitude through difficult situations or thoughts. Still, I want you to know this: Maintaining an attitude of gratitude is critical during tough times because it will help keep you moving forward. It will also give others hope when they see how happy you are with your life regardless of circumstances.

Gratitude means being thankful for everything, no

matter if we like it or not. And as hard as it may sometimes feel, maintaining a positive outlook on our lives can make us stronger and more resilient.

The key to feeling good again lies inside us—and as long as we keep looking for ways to feel better in ourselves instead of running from discomfort or trying harder at something else, we will be able to make progress one day at a time.

Remember, we have everything within us, and it starts with practice self-compassion now. Gratitude unlocks joy because it shifts your focus and energy when you see what is going right for you every day.

5) Balance is a myth. Stress is a sign that you need to put yourself first. Stress occurs when you expect one thing and get another. I permit you to put yourself first. It's okay. It's like on the airplane. They don't say put your mask on your kids and everyone else, and then put yours on!

They say to *put your mask on first* because if you don't have oxygen, you are no good to anybody. So, you must put the oxygen mask on like it's your fuel tank, like you are your number one priority. And over time, your family will start to see that that's what you're doing, that you need to put your mask on. But nobody's going to put it on your face. Nobody's going to go here, "You look a little low on oxygen." Let me give you mine. That's just not going to happen, especially for women. So, I would just say I permit you to put yourself first. I think a lot of women just need someone to say, "Hey sister, it's okay to just put your oxygen mask on."

6) Set boundaries. I am cautious about with whom I surround myself. This is simple – you become the average of the five people you spend time with – so make sure they are raising your game. Also, guard the door to your mind. That includes the news, movies, social media, negative input from other people around you. Currently in your life, it is critical to protect your space more than ever. Create a small inner circle of people who are compassionate and will lift your spirits.

Limit your time with people who don't support you. You are worthy of love and belonging, so if someone doesn't treat you that way, show them the door! It's not hard to do — it just takes some practice in being aware of how we let energy affect us. With awareness comes choice, and when there is a choice, it becomes easier to say, "No thanks."

As I regain my joy from deep inside me, I have found that I need less drama around me. My heart feels more open than ever before, and all those old voices telling me what I can't do or shouldn't be doing seem like they're coming from another lifetime ago.

7) Decide not to live in the past. That is the key. One of the critical components of joy is that joy is in the present moment and the future. Joy doesn't occur in the past. There was a moment I decided, "I refuse to replay the old movies of my past." When you see an awful movie, do you go watch it repeatedly? No! You don't! I don't live in yesterday. I don't live in three months ago. I live today, and I imagine an exciting, compelling, and empowering future.

Like right now in this present beautiful moment where my heart's beating; I'm breathing; I'm talking to you. I'm just in the moment.

So, I want to give you some ideas for things that will help you stop living in the past.

The first tip is to move toward something; don't just keep moving away from the past or what you can't control in life. Instead of being a victim and staying stuck in the pattern of pain that has been our story so far, start making small changes towards more pleasurable activities for yourself - no matter how small they may seem at first. Day by day, make small but essential decisions about where this new future might lead us all. Be careful not to attach too much meaning to those choices as we go along because it's tough to know sometimes if any decision made today was going to be right or wrong until we get there.

The second idea is that you can find joy in the small things again. There are so many ways to do this, and it depends on what makes you most happy, whether it's spending time with your family or taking walks around town on a sunny day. Find something every day and commit to doing it for yourself and no one else - even if only for a few minutes at first, but then build up from there as best you can!

The third way is simple. Just stop replaying that movie repeatedly. Period. It may be time to put the past behind you and move on.

There is a fourth way that I have found helpful in my own life: taking care of myself by eating well (incorporating lots of protein!) and getting enough rest. Practicing this helps me feel good about myself and keeps me from feeling stressed out - it's like giving yourself an energy boost! Sometimes when I am running low on sleep or tired, I'll take a break for 15 minutes and write down what I'm grateful for with color pens, so it makes me happy just looking at it later. I also love writing love letters to God. These letters are full of gratitude!

It never fails; whenever someone feels joy, they automatically smile more often because their mood improves! So, whatever you do today, start smiling more! The human brain will automatically associate smiling with being happy or feeling joy, which will help to boost your mood.

You can also try meditating for just a few minutes each day and journaling: both activities have been shown in studies to make people feel good about themselves, more creative, and healthier!

The last exercise I'll mention is taking time out for yourself - whether it's going on a walk with friends during the week after work or reading what you enjoy. Doing this makes me happier than anything else because I know that "me" time is essential. If we don't take care of ourselves first before we can provide happiness for others, then nothing will ever change."

<u>Joy</u> comes in the <u>morning</u>!

beyondbrave.
by jolynn swafford

A Warrior Fights the Good Fight

You have what it takes to fight the good battle!

If you got this far, then I'm proud of you. You are brave and bold! Keep fighting the good battle. We all need to know that we have what it takes inside of us to keep going when difficult times come our way. God is with us every step along the way, so never give up on yourself or your faith because there is always hope where there is life!

I know it may seem like the end of your rope is near sometimes, but I want you to remember all the good times when life seemed easy or even better- perfect. That's because those memories are what will help us keep on living for our family members who passed away; for ourselves so we can live out our dreams with renewed vigor; and finally, for others who need encouragement now and then too. We all have battles in life but don't forget: YOU WERE BORN BRAVE. You must never forget this.

Do not let anyone tell you otherwise. You were born to make a difference in this world, which takes bravery, faith, and love!

To fight the good battle, we must remember that life is a gift and not something owed. We also need to keep our minds set on higher things because this world has so many distractions (both good and bad). Lastly, remind yourself of all the difficult times you've come through before. That will give you bravery for whatever battles lie ahead!

The last thing I want people to know who are fighting their battles in life: YOU ARE BRAVE AGAIN AND ALWAYS WILL BE!!! You have overcome hard times before- there's no better reason than that to believe you'll do it again. The only question left is what your next brave act will be? Only time will tell!

I'm praying for you. Joy comes in the morning. Be BRAVE AGAIN!

You were born brave.

beyondbrave.
by jolynn swafford

Acknowledgments

The seeds for this work were planted in my heart by God. I am grateful that I even though I was once "lost", I am now "found" and can share my experiences and expertise with you now.

Without my husband, Eric Swafford, constantly encouraging me to write a book, this would have never happened. Thank you for being there for me, always. Thanks for leading bravely.

I also want to acknowledge and thank my daughter, Loren Hanson for braving the storm with me (especially in baba's last days). You are an incredible, generous force of light, I love you. Thank you for giving bravely.

And to Evan, my son, who also stood strong and even though he's an extremely busy, cool teenager, was never too cool to cry or give his mom a hug. Thanks for loving bravely.

To Kaylee and Lane Swafford, thank you for your love, support and prayers and for being there for all of us through thick and thin. I love you.

To my sister, Luan Cox, thank you for taking great care of our mom and dad. Mom lived a fulfilled life because of all of your travels together! I love you for supporting me and reminding me who I am (and was all along). Thank you for your grace and love.

To the Kenwards and my stepmother, Judy Cox and her sisters Babs and June, thank you for giving my dad a "home" and for loving him like you do.

To our warriors at Beyond Brave Co., Réne Baratella (our co-founder), Laura Harstad, Dan Wise, Loren Hanson, Todd Ross, Hrabren Bankov, you totally rock and inspire me to be a better leader every day. There is no way this book would have happened without your love, encouragement and hard work.

Finally, I want to thank my spiritual guides, mentors and pastors. Without you, I would stuck with just a bunch of ideas left undirected: Tim Storey, Paige Junaeus, Shane Gray, Paul Lambert, Tony Robbins and Brendon Burchard. You know how much I adore you. I thank you from the bottom of my heart and hope this book makes you proud of how far we've come together.

And thanks to Chief Gary Batton of the Choctaw Nation for being where God needs you.

Follow us!

Instagram:
@jolynnswafford
@beyondbrave.co

Join our #BraveArmy Community:
www.facebook.com/groups/beyondbraveonline

LinkedIn:
www.linkedin.com/in/jolynnswafford

Booking or Speaking Requests:
crew@beyondbrave.co

References

Hawkins, David, R. 2009. *Healing and Recovery.*

Hawkins, David, R. 2001. *The Eye of the I.*

Katie, Bryon. 2002. *Loving What Is.*

CPSIA information can be obtained
at www.ICGtesting.com
Printed in the USA
BVHW040050270621
610451BV00006B/1594

9 781006 884870